A Mystery to Be Lived

Dan Borgen

A Mystery to Be Lived

Published by Wheatmark®
2030 East Speedway Boulevard, Suite 106
Tucson, Arizona 85719 USA
www.wheatmark.com

ISBN: 978-1-62787-981-1
LCCN: 2022908979

Bulk ordering discounts are available through Wheatmark,
Inc. For more information, email orders@wheatmark.com or
call 1-888-934-0888.

Cover art, illustrations, and photography by Dan Borgen.
All author proceeds are donated to the Bedford-Stuyvesant
Volunteer Ambulance Corps in New York City.

CONTENTS

PREFACE

*Life is not a problem to be solved, but
a mystery to be lived.*
—Source undetermined

When my son, Miles, was around five years old, I asked him: "What's the meaning of life?"

He replied almost immediately with one word: "Death."

I've always found questions more compelling than answers. But that comeback stuck with me.

This little book is about life and death—and some of the main stuff that comes in between.

In different ways, it's a bit like life itself. It follows a few fundamental processes and organizing structures: grammar, words, sentences, and paragraphs. It's also based on a set of essential elements: letters, numbers, and punctuation.

Life doesn't come with a user guide. Neither does this book. You can plow through it as outlined or pick and choose things that might catch your attention. Since this is English, it seems reasonable to read from left to right rather than in reverse. Then again, according to Søren Kierkegaard, who's widely considered the world's first existential philosopher, life can only be understood backwards, but it must be lived forwards.

Like life, I'm not sure this book has any real purpose other than to experience it and hopefully enjoy at least some parts of it before, inevitably, it ends.

Like life, it also may appear somewhat random at times.

Like life, it's short . . . but if you find it horrible or uninteresting, it might *feel* long.

Like life, do with it what you will.

1

BIRTH

Who—or what—were you before you were born?

That seems as good a question as "What happens after you die?" But most folks do more existential head-scratching on the second query and little, if any, on the first—assuming they bother asking either one at all.

It's not as if preexistence is an imponderable that's never been pondered, though.

Questions persist.

Plato proposed that the process of being born wipes out all memory of previous life. Essentially, he believed we relearn everything we knew of our life before birth without attaining any new information in the process. . . *Is birth just redundant metaphysical recycling?*

The Jews, in their Book of Wisdom (also known as the Book of Solomon), lined up more or less with Plato's perspective. They just tended to tip their hat a little bit harder toward God. As time passed, though, the notion of preexistence, as well as an afterlife, became less of a normative position in Judaism. Their modern-day focus seems to lean more toward the here and now. . . *Is the question of preexistence mainly moot?*

The Christians don't share a unanimous stance on this topic. Some early adherents thought God created a soul for every upcoming human being. On the other hand, various Catholics, Eastern Orthodox, and Protestants supposedly subscribe to the Second Council of Constantinople's doctrine, which states, "If anyone asserts the fabulous preexistence of souls, and shall assert the monstrous restoration which follows from it: let him be anathema." So those folks seem pretty much opposed to the preexistence paradigm. The more recent Church of Jesus Christ of Latter-day Saints favors the term *premortal existence*, framed by the faith that human spirits have neither a beginning nor an ending. . . *Does that also apply to the Mormon underwear?*

The Baha'i Faith flock see life before life a tad differently as well. They posit that individual souls only arise at the time of conception and then become eternal thereafter. There's no preexistence from this position, although they make an exception for the founders of world religions like Buddha, Jesus, and Muhammad. The souls of those spiritual VIPs are believed to be preexistent. . . *Is there some sort of supernatural class system?*

The Hindus keep things somewhat simpler. Krishna allegedly claimed, "Never was there a time when I did not exist, nor you, nor all these kings, nor in the future shall any of us cease to be." Their creed embraces reincarnation—that all of life goes through a rebirthing cycle in the sea of *samsara* (a Sanskrit word for "flowing around") . . . *Do all souls swim in the same preexistence pool?*

The Buddha's teaching contrasts a bit with Hinduism. Although some Buddhist texts suggest previous births, the Buddha reputably taught of *anatta* (non-self). This way of thinking asserts that there's no permanent *atman* (self), or what others might refer to as a soul. There's only a stream of consciousness. . . *Do we all row gently down the stream, if not always merrily, merrily?*

According to Islam, all souls were created pre-existent and fully formed around the time Allah made Adam. But now the world's population is approximately eight billion people and growing every second. It's not clear where all these new souls are coming from . . . *How does the soul math work in this cosmic equation?*

I wonder . . .

It's worth noting that the accounts as described above may be potentially misleading, partially inaccurate, or completely wrong. The same could be said for portions of the chapters that follow. Specific parts might even piss some people off. I apologize if you're one of them. No offense meant. Really.

Regardless, where does this lead when examining the questions of preexistence?

It leads me, as almost everything does, to my favorite phrase in the English language:

I don't know.

I'll return to that refrain throughout the remainder of this book.

2

CHILDHOOD

Childhood is a magical time—until it isn't.

Looking back at childhood, it all flies by so quickly. Living through it day by day, it seems like it'll last forever.

Conventional psychology tells us there are five stages of child development. Some social sciences experts say there are six.

I wonder . . .

Is it hyperbolic to classify lesser forms of psychology as social "sciences" or as any kind of science at all? Chemistry is a science. Microbiology is a science. Some questionable fringes of psychological theory appear more like pseudointellectual spitballing.

But I digress . . . let's not throw out the viable theoretical babies with the psychobabble bathwater.

Moving along, here's a thumbnail sketch using common categories as an organizing framework.

According to academic cognoscenti, the standard five stages of childhood include:

1. **Newborn**: A newborn is completely dependent on its caregiver. The first couple of months of life center on eating, shitting, sleeping, and automatically responding to external stimuli. Newborns tend to start smiling at other people at

around three months, perhaps amused by their entrée into the magical play of life. At times they appear to be open awareness incarnate.

2. **Infant**: It's astounding how much happens in the process of becoming a one-year-old. Faces become familiar. Babbling begins. Head and hand and limb control increases. Crawling commences. Sitting up and standing start. The magic of pure awareness appears to morph into the sticky slog of ego identification. Infants first begin responding to a given name—from a blobby to a Bobby.

3. **Toddler**: The years between one and three signal self-locomotion and increasing independence. Standing, walking, running, and climbing. Waving bye-bye and holding implements. Drawing and communicating with simple words and phrases. Beyond basic response to stimuli, now the little one starts manipulating "reality" . . . whatever *that* is.

4. **Preschool**: From three to five, things start to get much more refined. From the blobness of babyhood, mini-people genuinely begin to emerge. Throwing and catching. Skipping and hopping. Dressing and toileting. The timeless magic lingers for a little while longer, although it slowly begins to fade away. At this stage, I can still recall being mesmerized, but somewhat less mystified, by dust particles surfing midair on sunbeams around the room.

5. **School age**: This phase is generally classified as ages six to seventeen. The ego increasingly solidifies into a sense of separateness. Formative experiences shape the drama and themes of life's storyline. Friendships may develop. Most dissolve over time. The same could be said for many remnants of the magic. Puberty ensues. Then sexual development—and, perhaps, obsession—shift into high gear. Some of us never seem to mature much

past that first hormone-fueled fascination.

But that comes later . . . so to speak. Sex is the topic for another chapter.

3

EDUCATION

Remember the misnamed "three Rs" of education: reading, writing, and arithmetic?

Maybe a more correct trio of consonants might instead be the three Cs: compete, consume, and conform. These frequently feel like the major messages of Western culture. And our American educational system often seems orchestrated in service to that socialization process—reinforcing a three-Cs cultural imperative from the time we start preschool.

But first, a timeout for full disclosure. I possess no formal qualifications of any kind to comment on pedagogy. I dropped out of high school at fifteen. Maybe I took a cue from Frank Zappa's sentiment, "If you want to get laid, go to college. If you want an education, go to the library." Plus, these days you don't even need to go to a library. Practically every facet of information is readily available online. On the other hand, getting laid at college has something going for it as well.

Again, I digress . . .

Our existing educational system is roughly two hundred years old. Before then, schooling was predominately reserved for the rich. But with the advent of the Industrial Revolution, factory bosses needed a sheeplike, obedient workforce. As Northwestern University economist Joel Mokyr puts it, "Much of this education, however, was not technical in nature but social and moral. Workers who had always spent their working days in a domestic setting had to be taught to follow orders, to respect the space and property rights of others, be punctual, docile, and sober."

Kids will always need to learn to be literate and know how numbers work. But do they need to be processed like submissive lambs on factory assembly lines? Where's the inspiration for critical thinking skills and skepticism? How can curiosity, a catalyst for learning, be nurtured? How can we transform the teacher's role from a sage on the stage into a guide on the side?

Bigger picture, maybe death is life's best professor. . . although pain might make a pretty good substitute teacher. Impermanence also often turns out to be the most essential course in everyone's existential curriculum.

May we all be lifelong learners.

4

SEX

I believe in being warm-hearted.
I believe especially in being
warm-hearted in love,
in fucking with a warm heart.
—D. H. Lawrence, *Lady Chatterley's Lover*

D. H. Lawrence nailed this one.

Of course, nowadays he might be faulted for a binary, male-centric, heterosexual bias. But it seems a bit unfair to place a twenty-first-century filter on an early twentieth-century novelist.

Regardless, I'm on board with his notion of "fucking with a warm heart." That's not to say a warm heart necessarily excludes spanking, sex toys, tahini sauce, or whatever else might strike the combined consensual fancy.

We're biological organisms. Accordingly, two major life forces propel us: survival and reproduction.

If we were eternal, without the drive to survive, there'd be no evolutionary reason for our species to generate offspring. No instinctual urge to replicate our genes. Yet all things do indeed die. So evolution not only sees to it that we do our best to stay alive. It also powers most of us with a potent lust to fuck.

Much of the time that compulsion isn't based on baby-making. But our genes don't know that. It just feels *so good*. And all the better if warm hearts are engaged in the action.

Warm hearts don't require a cosmic union of "soul mates" . . . whatever *that* means. Warm hearts may simply respect that there's another human being involved in creating what Shakespeare euphemistically referred to as "the beast with two backs."

There doesn't even necessarily have to be anyone else involved at all. Sometimes that's just, umm, the case at hand. In those situations, it might be worth embracing the sentiment of a famous (now culture-canceled) comedian who once quipped, "Don't knock masturbation. It's sex with someone you really love."

5

ADDICTION

A reciprocal relationship exists between pleasure and pain. Dopamine keeps score. There's no free lunch.

The Buddha is often quoted as saying that "life is suffering." Some might find that a dharmic downer. But it's worth noting the Buddha didn't speak English. He never uttered the word *suffering* at all. Purportedly, the word he used was *dukkha* (a Pali version of Sanskrit).

Dukkha encompasses much more. Although that term connotes pain and suffering, it also embodies the transient and ultimately unsatisfactory nature of *all* life experiences. So *dukkha* incorporates happiness and pleasure as well. They don't last forever either. The seesaw persists.

Life isn't always easy.

But we'd sure like it to be easier. We seek escape from *dukkha* in all its displays. Boredom, loneliness, low self-esteem, stress, heartbreak, jealousy, frustration. . . From these mind states and more, all types of addictions may come into play: booze, drugs, sex, cigarettes, work, gambling, video games, cell phones, social media, web surfing . . .

Can we dodge the *dukkha*?

Rumi, a Sufi poet and mystic from the thirteenth century, put this spin on it: "The cure for the pain is in the pain." We often prefer to anesthetize ourselves somehow. But does habitual numbing keep us from the wisdom our hearts genuinely hunger for? Maybe Rumi's suggesting there's a life-lesson gift of growth wrapped up in *dukkha*.

American medical doctor and scientist Robert Lanza developed an intriguing theory he calls *biocentrism*, which weaves together key concepts from astrophysics, biology, quantum mechanics, and neuroscience. One of its seven defining principles asserts that everything "dwells in an undetermined state of probability." From that perspective, I sometimes wonder if each moment also holds a small seed of choice among many possibilities. Over time, those choices might morph into habits. Those habits then may shape our lives.

You can't stay high forever—trust me, I've tried. Habitual escape just doesn't seem to serve me now. It's taken the better part of a lifetime to appreciate that, and I'm still learning.

There's no judgment in any of this. Quite the opposite. I'm actually a bit suspicious of anyone who's never altered their consciousness at some point along the way. Where's their curiosity?

But within this late stage of my own evolution, maybe I've arrived at some kind of supersaturation when it comes to seeking psychoactive solutions. Or perhaps I've just substituted my dopamine fix with healthier alternatives . . . like becoming a compulsive gym rat.

So now I'm apparently addicted to the habit of working out. It's ultimately a losing battle against entropy. But we'll confront that powerful thermodynamic force in the chapter on exercise.

6

CREATIVITY

Creativity is like water.

Water exists everywhere. It's in the atmosphere. Clouds are its most visible form up there. But even the air we breathe holds water in tiny atoms too small to see. The more obvious expressions of H_2O include oceans and lakes, rivers and streams. Water drops down from the sky in drizzling mists, splashy globules, and torrential monsoons. Or it shapeshifts into solids like ice or snow, vanishes into vapor, and then reemerges as a liquid. About 70 percent of our body is composed of water. More than 70 percent of earth is covered in it.

Creativity seems to swim in similar ways all around and within us.

Personally, I was uncertain how creativity might remain with me after I decided to stop making a living as a jazz trombonist. Yet throughout the remainder of my life to date, it's resurfaced in a variety of ways: art, acting, writing, singing, piano playing . . . even establishing and running small businesses.

I'm nothing special.

My sense is that everyone has creativity capacity—perhaps simply untapped. Creativity also isn't limited to the arts. Like water, it can take on myriad manifestations. People who say, "I'm not a creative person" may just be underestimating and misrepresenting themselves.

There's creativity in all the sciences. There's creativity in parenting. There's creativity in cooking, camping, caregiving, lovemaking, planning, gardening, budgeting, bullshitting . . . the list goes on and on.

Richard Dawkins was an Oxford-trained evolutionary biologist who wrote a thought-provoking and controversial 1986 book called *The Blind Watchmaker*. It contends that Darwinian natural selection is unconscious and automatic. Dawkins's basic premise was that if evolution played the role of nature's "watchmaker," it was blind—without purpose. Maybe he was right.

But is it possible that natural selection's watchmaker, although visionless and potentially purposeless, also might be driven by some unfathomable force that is—at its core—*creative*?

7

MONEY

Money—or the lack of it—dominates the minds and lives of many. It's also an international fiction.

That wasn't always the case. According to anthropologists, barter systems started over 100,000 years ago. Back then, most social groups relied mainly on gift-giving and debt, predominantly among tribe members. Barter was almost exclusively reserved for total strangers or possible adversaries. A little later, about 3000 BC, folks from the Americas to Australia started trading shells.

Researchers believe the first gold and silver coins didn't finally arrive on the scene until sometime between 650 and 600 BC. Then things got increasingly complicated. Commodities like gold and silver transformed toward a representative system. Banks and merchants started to issue paper money and banknotes as receipts for deposits, a concept first introduced by the Chinese. This set the gears in motion for the "gold standard," which backed legal paper with set amounts of gold. That standard was ultimately embraced by nearly everybody around the start of the twentieth century.

Several decades later, as the United States rose to global dominance shortly after World War II, most of the planet began to fix their country's currencies to the American dollar. But in 1971, the States stopped backing its buck's convertibility to gold. It didn't take long after that for many other countries to uncouple their native currency from the US dollar. In the process, they also stopped backing money to anything of real value besides a patriotic promise of the ability to trade it for goods and services.

Absent intrinsic worth, there was nothing to stop any governmental authority from simply printing more paper.

Paper money now seems so last millennium. In the twenty-first century, most funds exist in electronic form—floating invisibly across the ether among worldwide banking databases. On top of that, cryptocurrency is gaining traction. It's an entirely new medium of exchange built on computer-networked digits and capitalist-consensus reality.

Some people say money isn't important. Those are the folks who have enough of it. Although money may be a socially constructed global fabrication, it can quickly become a crucial one if you don't have at least a sufficient amount to feed, clothe, shelter, and support daily life.

Perhaps the most egregious aspect of money is wealth inequality. It occurs with individuals (I'm looking at *you*, Elon Musk and Jeff Bezos), within countries, and across multinational corporations. Apparently there's plenty of this fictional-yet-critical currency to go around. But greed, power, and systemic structures somehow keep the venal gears in perpetual motion. A tiny minority wildly prospers while large populations suffer needlessly.

My beloved grandmother Helen never had much money. She lived simply and quietly in a small time-worn studio apartment in New York City. Helen was fond of quoting this line by Somerset Maugham: "Money is like a sixth sense without which you cannot make a complete use of the other five."

Maybe she and her cited writer were trying to put money into perspective by prioritizing the richness of life experiences over the "stuff" that money can buy. Then again, that mindset may only be viable if you can clear the first hurdle of Maslow's hierarchy of needs: physical necessities. And that initial step still seems way too steep for far too many people.

When I visited Helen long ago, she'd cook dinner for us in her tiny Queens kitchen. I'd sit at

a small dinette table that barely squeezed behind her as she tended to the stove. Sometimes
she'd sing an old song from the 1920s while our
supper simmered. Lyrics about the moon, the
stars, birdsongs, and flowers mingled loving-
ly with the comforting aroma of chicken soup
and stuffed cabbage. Helen sang that song so
often it became embedded in my memory.

The name of that tune is "The Best Things in
Life Are Free."

. . . Priceless.

8

WORK

People periodically ask me for career advice. Sometimes I refer them to a related Venn diagram. I didn't invent it, but I've crudely recreated it here:

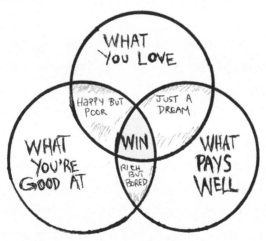

The diagram does an OK—but imperfect—job of capturing some of the major considerations related to vocation.

Despite what they might say, most folks really like money. But that doesn't make it the only driver. A singular focus on cash could lead to well-funded boredom or an unfilled fantasy. It's also probably desirable to like (if not totally *love*) what you do since you'll spend a large chunk of your life doing it. But if you're not competent enough to compete for good pay in the real-world marketplace, you might enjoy what you're doing yet face a lifetime of struggle.

The work circles interrelate and overlap. A central intersection of all three appears like an idealized scenario.

So what might be wrong with this picture?

Well, when looking at doing "what you love," many might be mind-fucked by the societal-pressure directive to "find your passion."

Is it possible that's ill-advised for a variety of reasons? Passions can change over time. People may also have more than one passion. Or they may not have any idea what their passion is at all. That might be fine. It doesn't necessarily mean something's *wrong*.

The cultural imperative to "find your passion" might also encompass a message of privilege and entitlement. A preponderance of people in the workforce simply don't have that luxury. They gotta eat.

Even if you're lucky enough to transform your passion into work, that passion may start feeling more like a job over time. It could lose the luster of its initial romance. Those sensations emerged within me after working for a while as a professional musician. Or, taken to an extreme, you might love having sex, but what if you had to do it all day, every day, with anyone who paid you for the service?

Most people have multiple jobs or careers throughout their lives. Each occupation presents an opportunity to learn and grow, although it may not feel that way at the time. Here's just a partial list of the things I've done for cash over the course of my lifetime to date: dishwasher, janitor, garbage collector, camp counselor, unskilled construction worker, slaughterhouse day laborer, lifeguard, musician, yoga teacher, scuba diving instructor, actor, management consultant, business owner, and walrus keeper.

Really. Walrus keeper.

Although I've done all those jobs listed above, none of them defines me. This may run counter to another common work-related mindset: career self-identity.

Work is something you *do*. But, at an intrinsic level, it's not who you *are*.

Some people live their lives as vocational hyphenates: Bradley Tarkington—Attorney, Sally McDougal—MD, Charles Farnsworth—CEO. For a percentage of folks like these, their professions can mutate into forms of addiction. Like a drug, work might serve to distract or numb them from chronic existential pain—or from getting to know their authentic selves, absent their job titles.

In a perfect world, that Venn diagram may also be missing a few other factors for consideration such as:

- Can the work make things a little better than they were before?
- Can the work be done with authenticity, curiosity, generosity, and empathy?

But it's not a perfect world.

Maybe, as a baseline, the best added work criterion should just be "do no harm."

Do fish know what it's like to be wet? They're entirely immersed in water, so it's unimaginable for them to notice it unless they leap beyond the surface. American culture seems to have a similar effect on its citizenry. That's one good reason for traveling outside the country now and then, if possible.

When visiting abroad, I like to ask the locals about their impressions of the United States. Along those lines, I'll never forget a brief conversation I had with an Italian cab driver many years ago. I asked him, "What do you think about Americans?" He paused for a very long time and then slowly replied in a thick Italian accent, "Their vacations are too short."

As a hospice volunteer, I've shared many intimate moments with folks shortly before they die. Every patient I've encountered taught me something about living. Maybe more than anything, though, they've reified an important reminder for me. Someday I'll be the one who's doing the dying.

Within that context, perhaps there's a reason some clichés have staying power. I've never heard anyone on their deathbed tell me, "I wish I'd spent more time at work."

9

RELATIONSHIPS

Here's a thought experiment. Let's call it the Relationship Game.

Imagine three cups:

1. The first cup is *you*. You're responsible for filling your own cup.

2. The second cup is the *other player*. They're responsible for filling their own cup, too.

3. The third cup is the *relationship*. Each player is responsible for periodically pouring some of what they've cumulated into the relationship cup.

It's delicious and life-affirming to drink from the relationship cup.

One player may sip a bit more than the other sometimes. It's not transactional. This isn't a competition. Neither player should keep score.

The game stops being fun when either player expects the other to make them happy. That's up to each participant. Players must continue to refill their own cups. Only then can each player pour freely into the relationship cup with genuine love, abundance, and generosity.

Relationship play becomes perilous (and neurotic) when one or both participants demand the other to "fill my cup!" That may end the game.

In other words, fuck *Jerry Maguire* and the rom-com fantasies he rode in on. "You complete me" is something a Hollywood scriptwriter made up.

For extended play, here's one more rule. Each participant must pour a fair share into the relationship cup over the course of the game. If only one does the preponderance of the pouring, that player's personal cup will inevitably become drained. Then the relationship cup can never truly be full.

10

FAMILY

A prominent British geneticist, mathematician, and evolutionary biologist named John Haldane was asked if he'd die for his brother. He reportedly joked back, "No. But I would willingly lay down my life for two brothers . . . or eight cousins."

In evolutionary terms, Haldane was alluding to the notion that if someone loses his life to save two siblings, four nephews, or eight cousins, each of these alternatives represents an equivalent "fair deal" from a DNA perspective. In averaged hereditary terms, siblings' genetic coding is 50 percent identical, nephews' 25 percent, and cousins' 12.5 percent.

But family is so much more than just genetics.

A page from Romanian history paints a horrific picture on that point. Nicolae Ceauşescu, the last Communist leader of Romania, enacted a decree in 1966 that banned both abortion and contraception for women younger than forty. Ceauşescu stated, "The fetus is the property of the entire society." The wrong-headed rationale behind this decree was his belief that an increase in population would fuel Romania's economic growth.

Unsurprisingly, Romanian birth rates soared over the next few years. Pairing population growth with poverty, increasing numbers of unwanted children were shipped off to state-run orphanages—places of institutional neglect, malnourishment, and abuse.

Decades later, after the West finally intervened, psychologists reported dramatic developmental deficits. Related cases included smaller body sizes, lower IQs, neurological and psychiatric disorders, abnormal development of social skills, and slow language acquisition abilities.

This tragedy highlights the undeniable requirement for children to have positive and supportive human connection.

A family can offer that sense of belonging, although that's not always so. In any case, families set the psychic stage with conditioning that informs and frames a child's initial worldview. Those values and principles lay the mental and moral foundation—positively, negatively, and everything in between. And maybe more than any words ever said, the behaviors modeled speak volumes.

No matter how the family cards are dealt, though, most folks spend close to the first eighteen years of life getting conditioned along these lines. Some might then spend the rest of their lives trying to undo much of that conditioning.

On a more upbeat note, families can also offer a priceless treasure: shared history—unique recollections only kin might share. Later, as parents and other relatives pass away, just a small and diminishing subset can retain those stories. Like other precious commodities, it's a bond that can become increasingly valuable over time.

These family fortunes may continue to grow and yield dividends through sustained investments in love and remembrance.

11

FRIENDS

Friends are the family you get to choose.

You're lucky if you find one good friend over the course of a lifetime. You're fabulously fortunate to have a handful.

These aren't Facebook friends. People who brag about having hundreds or thousands of friends on social media appear a bit delusional. Many of those "friends" only seem willing to display the highlight reels of a life façade.

True friends are the ones you share the best, the worst, and the rest with over the course of a lifetime. They love you throughout the journey without expectations, conditions, or scorekeeping. Together you encounter joys and sorrows, births and deaths. Their happiness is your happiness. Their pain is your pain.

There's a line from *Stand by Me*, a wonderful coming-of-age film about friendship, that resonated and stuck with me since first seeing it in 1986. The line goes like this:

"Friends come in and out of our lives, like busboys in a restaurant."

I've had the good fortune to develop and maintain meaningful, longtime friendships with a small crew of characters including an ex-con lawyer, a hillbilly multimillionaire, a clinically depressed bass player, an old hippie singer, and a former-Communist trumpet player. These connections have now survived more than several decades. I'd also be negligent not to include a diminutive, resourceful, and quirky Filipina among that intimate group.

She has been my wife—and a dear friend—for almost forty years.

I appreciate the many "busboys" who have entered and exited the table at my life's little restaurant. But I genuinely cherish the friends with staying power. They've helped serve a main course that's been nourishing and delicious beyond words.

12

PARENTHOOD

Being a parent is the best and hardest thing I've ever done.

Some people don't want to be parents. Their reasons can vary across a wide range of rationales: climate change, demise of democracy, financial insecurity, mental illness history, DNA abnormality, parental performance anxiety, intent to remain untethered, etc. I respect those folks who determine parenthood's just not right for them, irrespective of their logic. The world doesn't need any more unwanted kids.

But from an evolutionary perspective, there's a biological imperative for our species to reproduce. For many, it just seems like part of the ride on life's rollercoaster.

They'll need to strap in and hang on.

There is absolutely nothing logical or rational about the decision to become a parent. If anyone thought about it for too long, nobody would ever become one. The author Elizabeth Stone said, "Making the decision to have a child—it is momentous. It is to decide forever to have your heart go walking around outside your body." She was on to something. If you approach being a parent with a sense of purpose, you may never stop being one. The demands of the role change over time, but some part of that peripatetic parental heart keeps on pumping.

When my future wife and I first started dating, I shared a question with her that had been on my mind. I wondered, "Do I have the capacity to truly love?" Up to that point, I'd lived a largely solipsistic existence focused primarily on three things: I, me, and mine. My wife-to-be considered my query for a moment and then responded with her characteristic life wisdom, "You may never really know unless you have a child."

She was right. With the birth of my first son, a wellspring of love appeared as if out of nowhere and has never left. It altered me in such a profound way that I figured there just couldn't be any more.

I was wrong. With the birth of my second son, to my surprise, there was still plenty of love to spare buried somewhere deep inside me.

And then I was wrong again. By this point, I figured my love tank might be completely tapped out after becoming a father to two young sons. But a couple of years later, my baby daughter arrived. I wondered: did these kids access a seemingly bottomless reservoir of love submerged and hidden in my self-centered past?

Parenthood has dramatically transformed the way I look at the world and my place in it ever since.

Let's not sugarcoat this, though. The process has been far from effortless or trouble-free. For starters, there's parental fiscal panic. That drove me to work harder than I'd ever imagined. The US Department of Agriculture estimated that parents who had a baby in 2021 will spend, on average, close to $300,000 by the time that kid turns eighteen. In the early years, parenthood can also be physically exhausting. As the years progress, it then shifts to an emotional game. Maybe the things that make you craziest are those less-than-optimal aspects of yourself that you see repeated in your progeny. And let's also not understate the trials of parenting teenagers. The instructions to our impulse-control-addled teens ultimately boiled down to: "No hospitals. No police."

I applied teenagers to my hair; that's how it turned gray.

But there's also so much joy. I remember many years of happily rolling around on the carpet with three adorable, giddy youngsters. At the time, it felt like those days would last forever. Now they only exist in a cherished haze. You also never know what'll stick. It amazes me when my adult children echo small things I may have said or done in the past that they've selectively embraced now as their own.

Regardless, none of this ought to come with any expectations. Maybe that's a sane approach to life in general. But when it comes to raising kids, it seems particularly germane. Ultimately, it's their lives and life experiences. The best we can offer is love and support. Taking credit or blame for any related outcomes seems egotistical and wrongheaded.

When my own father reflected on his parenting style, I recall at times he'd repeatedly wail, "Where did I go wrong?" Then, as circumstances changed over the ensuing years, so did his tune. It modulated to "Well . . . I guess I must've done something right!"

I don't know . . . although I have a hunch, if you're lucky, your grownup offspring may become some of your favorite people in the whole wide world.

I'm lucky.

13

LEISURE

A friend of mine relayed a memorable conversation to me. Meeting his sister-in-law for lunch, she tried to initiate a chat with him by using America's cultural alternative of "how's it going?" She asked, "So are you keeping busy?" He promptly responded, "No. Not at all."

Banter became awkward between them after that.

Many seem to view "keeping busy" as a badge of honor, pride, or validation. It hasn't always been that way, though. According to anthropologists, our hunter-gatherer ancestors only worked about twelve to twenty hours a week to survive. They devoted the rest of their time to leisure. That was the norm until approximately twelve thousand years ago. Unlike the farmer, industrialist, and technocrat of future generations, the so-called savage enjoyed a lot more of their days just living life as a human being versus a human doing.

That's not to suggest a mass diaspora back to the jungle. It's not advocating indolence either. But research, experience, and observation indicate that all work and no play don't only make Jack a proverbial dull boy. They can also make him stressed, neurotic, unhealthy, and old before his time.

A previous chapter on the Relationship Game shared my cup-metaphor thought experiment. Well, here's an aphoristic cousin of that concept when looking at leisure: you can't pour from an empty cup.

Whether tending to children, studying for school, managing employees or your boss's expectations, caring for a dying person, or juggling a litany of other keeping-busy activities, we all need some me time for a refill. Some refer to this concept as *self-care*.

Self-care can take on as many different forms as there are folks who require it. Self-care can be meditation, but it doesn't have to be. Self-care can be reading a book, but it doesn't have to be. Self-care can be listening to music, but it doesn't have to be.

We all need time just to *be*.

Leisure also remains an unattainable luxury—a fantasy—for far too many. In our world of vast inequities and systemic deck-stacking, the very idea and attendant advantages of leisure time may come from a position of privilege.

So if you're one of the fortunate few, it might be worth considering the counsel of an American author, psychotherapist, and Buddhist teacher named Sylvia Boorstein: "Don't just do something, sit there."

14

EATING

There's a principle in writing called "the rule of three." Basically, it suggests that a triad of concepts, characters, or events is funnier, more memorable, and generally more pleasing than any other number. Think: the three little pigs, the three musketeers, or. . . a Christian, a Jew, and a Buddhist walk into a bar.

A rule of three also applies to principles of survival. On average, in priority order, humans can survive three minutes without air, three hours in extreme heat or cold, and three days without drinkable water. A person of normal weight might last for close to three months without food, if resting. Some extraordinary hunger-strikers have lived even longer.

Sleep is also critical to existence, but that's covered in an upcoming chapter. This one is about eating, an essential factor for life.

Obviously, we need food for basic nutrition and sustenance. But eating is so much more than just that. Meals can arouse all our senses, provide structure and anticipation to our days, convey love and social connection, keep traditions alive, bring back treasured memories, and characterize cultures.

Eating can be one of life's greatest pleasures. It can also lead to various forms of addiction, neuroses, and life-threatening illnesses. According to the Harvard School of Public Health, as of 2020, close to 40 percent of American adults aged twenty and over are obese. That number climbs to over 70 percent if you add adults categorized as "overweight" into the mix. On the positive side, however, being heavier may help out on a hunger strike.

I often look at life in general, and my own body in particular, as a kind of ongoing science experiment. When it comes to eating, I've conducted a variety of self-research studies along the way. I've been an omnivore, a vegetarian, a pescatarian, and a vegan. I've tried paleo, ketogenic, intermittent fasting, and Mediterranean diet styles. Currently, I lean toward the last one listed. For almost a decade now, I've also been doing a thirty-six-hour fast that coincides with the turn of each seasonal equinox or solstice. The fast isn't tied to any religion or doctrine. It's just my way of acknowledging each year's quarterly changes and performing a little physiological reset. Research suggests a whole bunch of health benefits attendant to fasting. But I'm not here to proselytize, so I won't blather on about that anymore.

Hippocrates, the ancient Greek physician, famously declared, "Let thy food be thy medicine and medicine be thy food." A less poetic and more modern version of that maxim is "Eat to live, don't live to eat." Then again, my uncle used to like to chide me during my vegetarian phase by saying, "We didn't claw our way to the top of the food chain for nothing!"

To each their own.

Some suggest eating lots less. In 1935, a scientist severely restricted the diets of lab rats. Purportedly, those rats lived up to 33 percent longer than previously thought possible. Related experiments followed over the ensuing decades, spanning species from worms to primates. They reduced caloric intake by as much as half the normal levels. The most favorable outcomes indicated the potential to extend life spans between 50 and 300 percent above average.

It's probably worth noting this was all done in a laboratory setting. Furthermore, humans are not rats. On top of that, as Lily Tomlin once quipped, "The trouble with the rat race is that even if you win, you're still a rat."

I. Don't. Know.

Caloric restraint may indeed be a key to longevity. Conversely, there's an old joke about extending life span into the triple digits that goes something like this:

A health-obsessed guy sees a doctor to inquire about becoming a centenarian. The man is instructed by his physician to drastically cut calories and abstain from all sweets, meats, eggs, dairy, salt, fries, gluten, and unhealthy fats. He's also advised to avoid risky hedonistic activities like consuming alcohol, taking recreational drugs, and having promiscuous sexual encounters.

The punchline? He may not actually live for one hundred years or longer . . . it'll just *feel* like he did.

15

NATURE

Nothing beats nature.

Words can only take us so far. The adjective *awesome* seems so overused that it's lost any real meaning. Nature defies description. Who hasn't looked up at a star-speckled sky and been dumbstruck with a true sense of wonder and awe?

Some people perhaps.

I used to be a frequent flyer. For a while, I commuted roundtrip on a weekly basis from Seattle to California. If the weather was right,

I got treated to fantastic birds-eye views of amazingly gorgeous volcanic terrain: Mount Shasta, Crater Lake, Mount Hood, Mount St. Helens, Mount Rainier. I can't forget a particular passenger who sat next to me on one of those flights. Seated by the window, I looked out and was graced by a picture-perfect, ice-cream-cone spectacle of Mount Rainier in all its shimmering glory. So I gently tapped the shoulder of my seatmate and pointed toward the prize I'd spotted to share it with him. He continued perusing his newspaper. Didn't bother to even look up. He just barely grunted back, "I've seen that before."

I remember thinking to myself, *I hope I never become so jaded.*

It hasn't happened yet. Although I've merely taken a nibble of nature's incredible banquet, I've been more fortunate than many and savored every taste. Some notable highlights include experiencing a total solar eclipse by a Pacific Northwest riverbank, marveling at the Northern Lights while standing on a frozen Arctic Sea, rappelling down roaring waterfalls in the foothills of Ecuador, witnessing the wonders of the Galapagos Islands, trekking in the snow-capped Himalayas of Nepal, exploring an underground river and caves in the Philippines, day-hiking to the bottom and back of the Grand Canyon, and scuba diving the ocean's depths among fantastically colored coral walls, reefs, and sea creatures.

But exotic isn't essential. Awe is accessible for anyone lucky enough to take a walk in the woods, dip a toe in a stream, glance at a glowing sunset, stroll along a lakeside, or look up at the moon.

It beats any painting, literature, music, sculpture, prayer, or poetry. It's nature—beyond-words beautiful. Or, as Trappist monk and social activist Thomas Merton put it, "Nothing has ever been said about God that hasn't already been said better by the wind in the pine trees."

16

EXERCISE

Entropy wins.

The second law of thermodynamics centers on entropy. In layperson's terms, entropy is the gradual and inevitable decline toward disorder. Science decrees that entropy always increases over time.

Life devolves into chaos.

When it comes to the body's journey over time, sarcopenia seems similar. *Sarcopenia* is the medical term for age-related muscle loss. According to Harvard MDs, sarcopenia starts in your midthirties. Left unattended, the typical person then loses muscle at the rate of around 1 to 2 percent each year. By the time folks turn sixty, the tempo picks up to approximately 3 percent each year after that. Based on statistical averages, people can expect to lose something like four to six pounds of muscle for every decade past their thirties if they don't take preemptive action.

Action is exercise.

I look at exercise a bit like flossing. My teeth and gums (and heart health) are invaluable, so I've made a habit of flossing every day. Floss comes in all kinds of forms: waxed, unwaxed, taped, threaded, mint-flavored, name brand, and generic. I've tried them all. Big picture, I'm not convinced it makes a huge difference which type of floss I use. *Habit matters*. Something just feels off if I don't floss. I sense the same about exercise. Over the course of my life, I've tried a variety of exercise: running, swimming, weightlifting, yoga, hiking, and rowing. Regardless of activity type, what's mattered is the habit of action.

Most experts concur that two basic forms of exercise are critical: aerobic conditioning and resistance training. I'm no expert—on anything. But I tend agree with them. I might also add two more: flexibility and balance exercises. Research indicates that one of three folks who are sixty-five or older falls every year. The CDC reports those trips land more than 800,000 of them in the hospital on an annual basis. Since more of us than ever before will live to be eighty or older, it just seems sensible to start moving, lifting, balancing, and stretching sooner than later.

Exercise also offers a potential smorgasbord of other health-related benefits. Studies suggest that the upsides include but aren't limited to improved memory and brain function, protection against chronic diseases, weight management, lowered blood pressure, improved heart health, better sleep, reduced depression, diminished anxiety, lessened joint aches, and increased life span.

Lots of people rely on their cars to get around. Some may own multiple cars over the course of a lifetime. But you only get one body. Maintenance seems essential for keeping both in working condition, although there are no guarantees for either over the long term. When it comes to cars, you can change the oil, rotate the tires, and replace the spark plugs. But cars can still break down. It seems comparable for our bodies. We can eat well, get sufficient sleep, and exercise every day. But the body can still break down too. For example, just last year, I experienced a detached retina. My headlight went out.

Entropy wins.

Despite what some futurists may tell us, none of us will live forever. Exercise isn't a panacea. It's no assurance of an extended life span—the years in our life. But it still may be the best bet for a positive health span—the life in our years.

17

SLEEP

Most folks know we spend approximately one third of life asleep. As of 2019, the average life expectancy in the United States clocked in at about seventy-nine years. That means the typical US citizen spends well over twenty years either unconscious or dreaming . . . although these snoozy brain states may be considerably higher for many Americans, figuratively speaking.

What may be even more interesting, though, is that the scientific and medical communities are just now beginning to comprehend why we sleep at all.

Three of our bodies' basic biological drivers seem obvious to most: eating, drinking, and reproducing. But sleep, a fourth physical imperative, remains somewhat mysterious.

From an evolutionary view, did you ever wonder . . . why would our species spend so much time over the course of human history unable to find and consume food? Why make us too comatose to hang out, date, mate, and raise our kids? Wouldn't slumber also make our paleolithic ancestors easy prey for predators?

But, man, we *need* sleep. According to neuroscientist Matthew Walker in his book *Why We Sleep*, "the shorter your sleep, the shorter your life. The leading causes of disease and death in developed nations—diseases that are crippling health-care systems, such as heart disease, obesity, dementia, diabetes, and cancer—all have recognized causal links to a lack of sleep."

Sleep's necessity hasn't been lost on the US intelligence community either. In 2003, CIA general counsel Scott Muller wrote an email declaring "CIA headquarters informed CIA detention sites . . . that sleep deprivation over 48 hours would now be considered an 'enhanced' interrogation technique." That's fed talk for another term: *torture*.

While it's still not entirely clear *why* sleep is so incredibly important, it's increasingly apparent *what* it does for us. Researchers now tell us that sleep boosts our immune system, helps prevent weight gain, can enhance cardiovascular function, improves mood, upgrades exercise performance, strengthens memory, and cleans out toxins in our brains.

Arthur Schopenhauer, an eminent German philosopher, put all of this in existential financing terms: "Sleep is the interest we have to pay on the capital which is called in at death; and the higher the rate of interest and the more regularly it is paid, the further the date of redemption is postponed."

It also just *feels* so damned good.

18

SERVICE

Service seems integral to a life well lived.

It's also ultimately one of the most self-serving things I've done with mine. Over the years, I've engaged in a wide variety of volunteer activities, including but not limited to working as a hospice volunteer, serving as a crisis counselor, mentoring aspiring entrepreneurs, teaching English as a second language, being a Big Brother, serving meals to folks facing homelessness, participating on the boards of nonprofits, and developing strategic plans for arts organizations in my local community.

This isn't virtue signaling. These are all shadow shapes of selfishness.

In every instance, serving others made me happier, helped me learn, and supported my personal growth.

If I had to pick one area that's fed me the most, though, I'd say it's been hospice volunteering. Hospice has provided me with the privilege of gently connecting with a wide range of people. It's given me a sense of what it means to grow old, become sick, and die. This form of service continues to offer a profound education with every patient I encounter. . . The repeated, remedial lesson? Someday the very old man on his deathbed will be me. That's if I'm lucky.

But the concept of service isn't limited to formal volunteering pursuits. It also means being there for family and friends, for neighbors and acquaintances, for clients and customers. In these ways, service can range from just lending a helping hand to simply *listening* with supportive, undivided attention.

Compassion makes a good compass. And actively listening may be one of the most meaningful services of all.

According to the Mayo Clinic, volunteering also improves physical and mental health, provides a sense of purpose, teaches valuable skills, and nurtures social connection. It can ward off loneliness and depression. A Carnegie Mellon study also found that volunteering on a regular basis correlated to lower blood pressure. It can mitigate the risks of heart disease, stroke, and premature death. Put another way, service might help keep us alive.

Setting aside any personal benefits that might ultimately accrue, some studies also suggest that *intention* matters. A 2012 report in the *Health Psychology* journal indicated that regular volunteers lived longer if their primary intentions were genuinely rooted in helping, not just centered on feeling better about themselves.

I don't know.

Maybe Muhammad Ali said it best and most eloquently: "Service to others is the rent you pay for your room here on earth."

19

CONSCIOUSNESS

Are you aware of being aware?

Consciousness seems to be at the center of what it means to be alive. It underlies all experience. It's also baffled the minds of men and women for millennia.

Some modern-day philosophical cognoscenti refer to "the hard problem of consciousness." They suggest that we might someday be able to explain away all the "easy" problems of awareness through empirical understanding of the brain's physical systems and biomechanics that enable sensation, information integration, and discrimination. But the hard problem endures.

The hard problem pivots on subjective experience—a singular point of view. For example, what's it like for *you* to experience the color red? What does an orange taste like? Or, as the philosopher Thomas Nagel asked, "What is it like to be a bat?"

Theories abound regarding the nature of consciousness. But at a reductionist level, all of them have two primary parents: monism and dualism. The ancient Greek philosopher Plotinus is one of the earliest mothers of monist belief. Basically, this concept asserts that "all is one" and everything is explainable as a single reality. The mind and the brain are the same thing from this point of view. The counterargument, dualism, was most famously fathered by René Descartes with his statement "I think, therefore I am." Some other ancient Greeks also had a few dialectic pups on the dualism side of this dogfight. Dualism contends that the mental and the physical are two very different entities.

These two theories gave birth to a large and varied litter of philosophical offspring. In the monism camp, for example, there's pantheism, which posits that everything is God. On the dualistic flipside, there's animism, which purports that everything material is made alive and conscious at some level by an invisible force like a soul. More recently, some neuroscientists and quantum physicists have revived an interest in panpsychism, which proposes that consciousness is a kind of fundamental, subatomic feature of reality that exists throughout the universe. There are also other modern-day academics who forward the notion that consciousness is akin to an electromagnetic field and that our brains work a bit like biochemical radio receivers.

Names may change, but the metaphysical melody lingers on. Among the new-age crowd, *nondualism* now appears to be a top-ten term on the spirituality hit parade. But the concept has been around for a very long time. It's basically monism rebranded, derived from the centuries-old Hindu philosophy of Advaita Vedanta. It's also been taught in some Buddhist and Taoist schools. Currently, there's a myriad of mindfulness pseudo-gurus on the spirituality lecture circuit pitching nondualism and asserting with solemnity that "everything is consciousness." On the other end of the continuum are the science-based materialists, whose view is that consciousness is the epiphenomenon, a byproduct, of brain and body processes. For them, mind is animated meat.

Stumbling deeper down this ontological rabbit hole . . . is awareness itself what gives rise to the sense of "I"?

Physician and philosopher John Locke thought so. He was the first to define the self as a "continuity of consciousness." Quite a contrarian for the seventeenth century, he rejected the idea that personal identity is the stuff of body or soul. From his perspective, "I" is a construct of consciousness made real only by memory.

Then again, the self-proclaimed philosophical entertainer Alan Watts once said that "trying to define yourself is like trying to bite your own teeth." Maybe what he meant is that you can obtain a partial understanding, but you can never fully grasp the entirety. Consciousness may be similar.

I remember attending a ten-day silent meditation retreat years ago on a beautiful island in British Columbia, Canada. Throughout the retreat, we were instructed to meditate with "choiceless awareness." Somewhere along the line, I became consumed by a question that surfaced persistently throughout many of my silent moments: what *is* awareness?

At the conclusion of each evening's dharma talk, the speakers expounded upon topics of interest that retreatants had been invited to write down in advance. This retreat featured a prominent meditation master known for popularizing Buddhism in the West. One night, that teacher responded to the question I'd submitted. Softly, slowly, and serenely, he read aloud, "What is the nature of awareness?" And then, with great authority, he informed the attentive roomful of retreatants, "Empty cognition."

Hmm . . .

Ever-curious and still uncertain, I was later led by independent exploration to learn about mysterianism. I'm not making that word up. That's really what it's called. And its adherents are known as mysterians.

Mysterians take the position that the hard problem of consciousness can't ever be cracked by mere mortals. In other words, like Alan Watts's metaphysical dental enigma, they believe our intellectual abilities have limitations and boundaries. Their take is that some mysteries are beyond our comprehension. They think we'll *never* know what awareness is or how it works. To them, our primate brains can only take us so far.

Another wise and famous philosopher, Groucho Marx, declared, "I refuse to join any club that would have me as a member." I've never been much of a joiner either. But if absolutely forced to subscribe to one specific school of consciousness epistemology, well . . . maybe sign me up with the mysterians?

20

LOVE and FEAR

Here's another thought experiment. Picture this: Place all emotions on a continuum with fear on one end and love on the other.

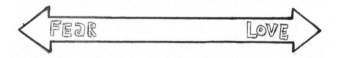

Could we distill each endpoint down to its respective essence as a fear of death and the love of life?

I wonder . . .

Are hate, greed, egotism, anger, arrogance, worry, and deceit just different shades of fear? Do they all fuel a primal drive for self-preservation?

On the other hand, could all of love's colors be life-affirming hues like compassion, humility, generosity, patience, honesty, calmness, and joy?

The word *love* is so overused and misused, though. It's almost lost real meaning. Maybe the ancient Greeks were on to something by breaking down the concept of love into more descriptive categories. The Grecian formula looked like this: *eros* (sexual passion), *philia* (deep friendship), *ludus* (playful love), *agape* (love/compassion for everyone), *pragma* (long-standing love), and *philautia* (love of the self).

Words are fascinating, but they aren't the thing itself. As Bruce Lee said in *Enter the Dragon*, taking his cue from the Buddha, "It is like the finger pointing to the moon."

Put another way, you might focus on the finger, or the word, and miss seeing what's truly authentic about the moon, knowing it intrinsically for yourself.

Language can also offer insightful clues about what's most important to a culture. For example, some researchers claim that Inuit languages have close to fifty different words for *snow*. And in English, there are easily over a hundred slang expressions for *penis*, including some rather obscure ones like *baloney pony*, *one-eyed Willie*, and *heat-seeking moisture missile*.

But, again, I digress . . .

Anyway, it seems like we all may be water-skiing on this fear-love continuum, riding the waves of emotions between its opposing ends.

In *Hamlet*, William Shakespeare tells us, "There is nothing either good or bad but thinking makes it so." There might be some truth to that. But we can also overthink things.

Under certain circumstances, fear and its psychological cousins may provide a necessary function. Like growth, for instance.

I've known long-time meditators (including myself) who, for periods of points on "the path," seemed to dismiss or detach themselves from the darker sides of their personal fear-love teeter-totters. There's a name for that process: *spiritual bypassing*. The phrase was first launched into play in the mid-1980s by a psychotherapist named John Welwood, who defined it as a "tendency to use spiritual ideas and practices to sidestep or avoid facing unresolved emotional issues, psychological wounds, and unfinished developmental tasks."

So when fear's partners in pain show up at our doorstep, it may not be such a bad idea to welcome them inside rather than attempt to escape or push them away. We might be shutting ourselves off to real riches on the other side of the continuum. Maybe life is offering the challenge and encouragement to make like a curious, kindly scientist—to keenly observe, explore, and examine some specific aspects of worry, anxiety, and discomfort within us.

If we try ignoring them, they'll probably just keep on knocking at the door anyhow.

21

RELIGIOUSNESS

The most beautiful thing we can experience is the mysterious . . . He to whom the emotion is a stranger, who can no longer pause to wonder and stand wrapped in awe, is as good as dead—his eyes are closed . . . To know what is impenetrable to us really exists, manifesting itself as the highest wisdom and the most radiant beauty, which our dull faculties can comprehend only in their most primitive forms—this knowledge, this feeling is at the center of true religiousness.

—Albert Einstein

Buddha wasn't a Buddhist. Christ wasn't a Christian.

In music, true artists acquire a uniquely distinctive sound. Some may learn from these masters as part of their personal development. But unless and until they discover their *own* voice, they'll be mere facsimiles at best.

I wonder if religiousness works in a similar way.

That doesn't mean organized religions serve no purpose. People love stories. And religions provide lots of nice stories. People also crave answers to inexplicable questions. And, God knows, religions offer a bunch of authoritative answers. People hunger for a sense of community as well. Likewise, religions create community for many in meaningful ways.

Most religions also endorse some version of the Golden Rule. And who can argue with treating others as you'd like to be treated? Or, said simply, try not to be an asshole.

But some of these pious societies foment a demonization of the "other." For instance, although Gandhi was deeply moved by Christ's Sermon on the Mount, he was disgusted by blatant segregation practices of the church. Consequently, he proclaimed, "I'd be a Christian if it were not for the Christians."

You really don't need a degree in history to discern that many of the most heinous acts of all time can be linked to religion. Just peek under the cult covers. There you might find power plays, corruption, greed, abuse, misogyny, fearmongering, and control of the masses all masquerading as righteousness.

From my own admittedly limited and biased perspective, organized religions seem to have caused more harm than good. Is Genesis the genesis? Supposedly that's where God said humankind should have "dominion over the fish of the sea, and over the birds of the air, and over the cattle, and over all the wild animals of the earth, and over every creeping thing that creeps upon the earth." I'm looking at *you*, climate change.

But keep the religious art, music, and architecture. A lot of that stuff's divine.

Some others may attempt to evade denominational monikers by proclaiming, "I'm *spiritual*, but I'm not religious." You say "potato"; I say "potato."

I don't know.

Once again, maybe impermanence is the greatest guru. Many Eastern religions and so-called spiritual teachers also point in that direction as a key to enlightenment . . . whatever *that* means. But can we leave all the seeking and dharma talk at the door? Can we just experience, wonder at, and embrace the mystery of life's passing moments for ourselves?

Maybe then there's no need for God, religion, enlightenment, or anything else.

The end of seeking . . . *Is-ness.*

Sometimes people ask me, "Are you a Buddhist?"

Nope. At best, I'm a be-ist.

22

ATTITUDE

Neutral seems vastly underrated.

Attitude apparently plays a big part in shaping the way we live and look at our lives. Within this context, some folks like to trot out the old question "Is the glass half full or half empty?"

To that I say, "Bullshit."

Technically, the glass is always full. Half of it's liquid; the other half is air. So it's never really empty.

The glass is refillable. So there's that.

You've got a damned glass. So where's the gratitude for having one at all?

"How's it going?" and "How are you?" are common greetings. I often have a strong suspicion that folks really don't want an answer, though. They just may feel compelled, on autopilot, to mutter some social-norm salutation. Regardless, my standard response is "fortunate and grateful." That's a baseline for me.

This doesn't mean my life's perfect. Far from it. I have preferences and disinclinations like anyone else. But I do feel lucky and thankful just to be alive.

It's a bit like the weather. Atmospheric conditions change all the time. I might prefer a warm, sunny day to a cold, wet one. But I still appreciate having the experience of whatever meteorological conditions might arise . . . versus none at all.

Pema Chödrön, an American Buddhist nun,

put this spin on it: "You are the sky. Everything else—it's just the weather."

I've got a glass.

In his 1946 book *Man's Search for Meaning*, Viktor Frankl chronicled his experiences as a Nazi death camp inmate during World War II. A key quote from that memoir encapsulates one of its major contentions: "Everything can be taken from a man but one thing: the last of the human freedoms—to choose one's attitude in any given set of circumstances, to choose one's own way."

Maybe that worked for Viktor. But I'm doubtful it does for everyone. I'm not convinced it's always possible to "choose one's attitude." Who (or what) is doing the choosing anyway?

The Talmud tells us, "We do not see things as they are; we see them as we are."

Science has learned a lot about brain neurochemistry since Frankl crafted his 1946 thesis.

We continue to discover more every day. Science now tells us that all neurotransmitters are not created and distributed equally, particularly when it comes to key mood influencers like dopamine, norepinephrine, and serotonin. On top of that, other factors like genetics and childhood conditioning can play considerable roles in our habitual mindsets.

Also, just for the record, it's physically impossible to pull yourself up by your bootstraps. What a dumb-fucked expression. Go ask Newton and Galileo about gravity.

The gravity of life itself seems heavier for some than others. People in psychic pain might require the assistance of a qualified professional or prescription just to help drag their feet an inch off the existential ground—or lift heavy heads above muddy emotional waters.

To them I say, "*Whatever works.*"

23

AGING

Here's a three-act script for your inner voice across the main stages of life:

- **Act 1:** "I'm worried what everybody thinks about me."
- **Act 2:** "I don't care what anyone thinks about me."
- **Act 3:** "Hey . . . nobody's thinking about me!"

One of my former hospice patients, Gene, spent most of his life working as a farmer. He toiled long and hard in the Pacific Northwest. To me, Gene was like an old Zen master.

I visited with him at the assisted living facility where he resided. Gene was extremely hard of hearing and mostly immobile. He also had kind eyes, a warm smile, and a surprisingly strong handshake.

On one memorable visit, Gene told me he wasn't sure how old he was. I reminded him that he was 103. He said, "That's old."

I agreed. Then I asked him what he thought was the most important thing he'd learned in all those years. Gene thought for a moment and softly answered, "Don't worry."

We laughed.

I told him he'd lived much longer than me and that I valued his wisdom. I asked him what he thought was the most important thing he could teach me.

Gene considered this question in silence, seemingly at a loss for words, and then slowly replied, "Let it go."

Nobody ever said aging was easy. Bodies sag; memories fade; people you love die.

Curiously, though, aging isn't a given for every creature in the animal kingdom. Scientists have discovered a few species that, theoretically, can live forever—absent predation, accidents, or malevolent marine biologists. They appear not to age at all. These beings include a certain kind of jellyfish (*Turritopsis dohrnili*), hydras (small, tubular freshwater organisms), tardigrades (eight-legged micro-animals also known as "water bears"), and lobsters. They all possess truly remarkable regenerative abilities we mere mortals can only dream about.

But would you want to be a lobster?

Other research indicates that castrated men live, on average, fourteen years longer than uncastrated men accounting for general similarities in all other factors. In fact, it seems that the younger you're castrated, the longer you live—sometimes by as many as twenty years.

But would you want to be a castrato?

As far as we know (which really isn't much), humans are the only species with an awareness of our own mortality. Many prefer not to think about it.

When we're young, we understand on an intellectual level that aging exists. But it carries a somewhat remote and distant quality. It's almost as if we tell ourselves, "Old age happens . . . to other people." That mindset doesn't last if you live long enough, though.

Then again, there may also be some upsides to aging.

In classic psycho-jargon, a Stanford professor named Laura Carstensen developed something she christened *socioemotional selectivity theory*. It postulates that as our perceived time horizons diminish, we prune down our lives in ways that focus on, prioritize, and invest in emotional meaning, connections, and positivity.

Another study from the *Journal of Clinical Psychiatry* analyzed data from over fifteen hundred people ranging in age from twenty-one to ninety-nine to assess physical, cognitive, and mental well-being. As you might expect, the elderly displayed more physical and cognitive deterioration. Surprisingly, though, the older folks also appeared to be the happiest. Conversely, participants in their twenties and thirties reported the greatest degrees of depression and stress—and the lowest feelings of fulfillment.

Does this mean that those almost-immortal lobsters are incredibly cheerful crustaceans? Are the long-lived, deballed male sopranos considerably more upbeat?

Curiouser and curiouser . . .

Like Alice in my own wonderland, that leads me to one more nugget of wisdom I received from another old guy I knew. By chance and good fortune, I became friends with a nonagenarian in my neighborhood. Chuck had been an editor, then publisher, of our local community journal for over three decades. Not long before he died at the age of ninety-eight, I asked him what led to his extreme longevity. Chuck reflected for a moment and told me, "You know, I was a newspaper man for many years . . . I was always curious about everything going on around here . . . I'd have to say . . . curiosity."

So with love and gratitude for a departed reporter and a fallen Zen farmer, maybe these are three key ingredients for an aging-well recipe:

- Don't worry.
- Let it go.
- Stay curious.

24

TIME

Does anybody really know what time it is?

Concepts abound. But no one definitively *knows*. According to the best definition classical physics can offer us, time is "what a clock reads."

Then Albert Einstein came along, looked at time sideways, and got the whole world thinking about it differently. He famously forwarded the idea of an inextricably linked "space-time" in his theory of relativity. Einstein viewed space-time as a fourth dimension in which the perception of past, present, and future can differ depending on the comparative position or movement of observers.

And that's just for starters. Some modern-day theoretical physicists, like Carlo Rovelli, think time is an *illusion*. That notion surrounds a current theory called *loop quantum gravity*. Its intent is to unify quantum mechanics and general relativity. Rovelli's view is that what we call *reality* is just networked events governed by laws of quantum mechanics and thermodynamics. What we perceive as "time" seemingly appears to materialize for us from that scientific stew. Put another way, we project a sequence through our senses—but the "arrow of time" isn't real.

The idea of time's arrow is something we all can relate to on a visceral level, especially as our bodies age. It maps to our shared experience that time is a one-way street. But the arrow of time continues to be an unsolved physics problem. Or maybe it's just a matter of perspective.

It's been said that we don't age because there's time; we age because there's change.

Another hypothesis, called the *block universe theory*, proposes that the cosmos is a gigantic, infinite four-dimensional hunk of space-time composed of everything that ever happened and ever will happen—anywhere, at any time. From this viewpoint, the past, present, and future all exist simultaneously, and all are equally "real."

Perhaps, once again, the ancient Greeks were on to something. They had two different words for time: *chronos* and *kairos*. It's Greek to me, but one way to distinguish them might be to look at this type of time semantics metaphorically as different kinds of water. *Chronos* time is a flowing river that carries us forward and away. *Kairos* time is a quiet lake that we float or swim in. So . . . quantity versus quality, minutes versus moments, a watch versus a window.

Whether real or imagined, time appears to play an important role in all our lives. It also may raise one more question: is time travel possible?

I wonder . . .

Occasionally, I experience a personal version of time traveling when I'm around my three adult children. They're all in their thirties now. But once in a while when I look into their eyes or catch an inimitable expression, time travel can happen for me in a flicker. I suddenly see them as seven or seventeen, ten or three, eight or eighteen, and then back to the present again.

That's my favorite kind of relativity.

25

DEATH

Exercise regularly. Eat sensibly.
Die anyway.

— Anonymous

Is dying inevitable? If not, should it be?

A study cited in *Nature* journal put it like this:
"Current understanding of the biology of aging points firmly away from any idea that the
end of life is itself genetically programmed."

Researchers from across the globe now are
questioning whether any limit exists at all

once we discover how to control the diseases that kill us.

At the University of Rome, mathematician Elisabetta Barbi analyzed thousands of Italians who lived to be 105 or older. She determined, from a statistical perspective, that if you can make it past 104, your risk of death in the upcoming years plateaus at around 50 percent— counter to the standard dying-risk trajectory that accelerates as you age.

Siegfried Hekimi is a pioneering PhD in the biology department of McGill University who specializes in manipulating genes and mitochondria to extend life-span longevity. He applauded Barbi's work. To sustain levelized death rates like these, Hekimi hypothesizes that our cells may ultimately arrive at a place where the body's healing processes counteract many of the typical impairments associated with aging.

So how far can you extend life's expiration date?

Aubrey de Grey, a biomedical gerontologist and author of *The Mitochondrial Free Radical Theory of Aging*, theorized to the *Financial Times* that someday we all could live to be one thousand years old through medical technology... And if that's true, brides and grooms may start seriously reconsidering the "till death do us part" clause of their wedding vows.

They needn't worry too soon, though. Reputable scientists from around the world have discredited de Grey's analysis. As cultural critic H. L. Mencken allegedly quipped: For every complex problem there is a solution that is simple, direct, understandable—and wrong.

Can we know day without night? Hot without cold? White without black? Can we truly know life without death?

I like to keep death lightly on my shoulder, quietly whispering its mortality reminders into my ear. This isn't a morbid mindset. Death makes living more real for me. It's also not a novel idea. Purportedly, Plato's final instruction to his disciples shortly before his own life ended was "Practice dying."

These days, yammering on about living in the moment seems almost cliché. Eckhart Tolle made a fortune extolling "the power of now." But death doesn't need modern-day gurus promoting the present on talk shows. Death can tell us every day, every instant, to pay attention and appreciate the priceless gift of just being alive.

Death is also something we all share in common. It doesn't care if you're a man or a woman, gay or straight, American or Armenian, a janitor or a CEO. That commonality can offer connection.

I've literally spent thousands of hours in meetings over the past several decades. And it would be wildly disingenuous to describe all of them as persistently scintillating. So sometimes I'd look at each face around the conference room table and think to myself, *Like me, this person will die one day*. I concede that might sound strange. Just to be clear, though, this wasn't a death wish. It probably didn't serve the meeting's agenda very well either. But it boosted my compassion. It shook me out of business-is-business boredom. It rang a psychic wakeup call—an alarm bell for my awareness.

Death can also bring sadness. You miss your loved ones when they die. To some, it seems unfair.

So people have been trying to make sense of mortality for centuries. Customs surrounding death vary across the globe. For example, Mexican culture defines three kinds of death:

1. When you first realize intellectually that you will die

2. When you are physically dead and buried

3. The last time someone says your name

The first chapter of this book examined the question of life before life. It summarized a few prevailing views on that topic. Despite a temptation to end this penultimate chapter with a reciprocal spin on life after death, I won't go there. It appears to me like much of that would be redundant. All of it would be conjecture.

That's another thing about death: it's the ultimate personal adventure. No one knows with absolute certainty where death leads. Sure, some may point to myriad accounts of near-death experience (NDE). But here's the thing about NDEs: the phrase itself includes the word *near*.

Maybe *The Princess Bride*, a fantastic film from the '80s, best captures that essence of NDEs. Miracle Max the Wizard makes a big distinction between near dead and completely dead, emphasizing that *mostly* dead is still slightly alive. He concludes that there's typically only one thing you can do with someone who's *all* dead. "Go through his clothes and look for loose change."

Folks have been chasing immortality for thousands of years—as long as recorded history. *The Epic of Gilgamesh* is an ancient Mesopotamia series of poems and legends, with estimates of its origins dating back to 2100 BC. It's regarded by many as the earliest surviving form of literature. Second only to some sacred findings unearthed in the pyramids, it also happens to be one of the oldest religious texts. The core plot surrounds the death of Gilgamesh's dear friend followed by a related quest to overcome old age, sickness, and death. In the end, Gilgamesh doesn't attain everlasting life—but he does become a wise and renowned king.

Most historians believe there actually was a real person named Gilgamesh who ruled as the king of an ancient Sumerian city-state. So, according to the Mexican three-deaths taxonomy, perhaps Gilgamesh eventually achieved a kind of immortality after all. We're still saying his name.

But enough with the arts. Let's get back to science . . .

The Big Bang theory tells us that carbon, nitrogen, oxygen, and all the other atomic elements that make up our bodies were created in the stars billions of years ago. Science says that all gets recycled after we die. A gigantic carbon-based celestial circuit.

Astronomer Carl Sagan put this more poetically and took it one step further by saying, "The cosmos is within us. We are made of star-stuff. We are a way for the universe to know itself."

Maybe . . .

26

CONCLUSION

We know so little—and understand less.

For starters, what constitutes close to 96 percent of the cosmos? The smartest astrophysicists in the world are unable to formulate an empirical answer to that question. The most sophisticated quantum theories and cutting-edge tools can't tell us.

To put this in more technical terms, according to science journalist Richard Panek, who specializes in topics related to space and gravity, "The overwhelming majority of the universe is: *who knows*?"

Cosmologists invented two placeholder names in an attempt to start unpacking this enigma: *dark matter* and *dark energy*. Hypothetically, dark matter accounts for approximately 27 percent of matter in the universe to help explain how gravity can work in the vastness of space without the existence of some unseeable, unfathomable . . . stuff. Dark energy is the name they gave to roughly 68 percent of the remainder pieces to this intergalactic puzzle. It's a mysterious force that's causing the expansion rate of the cosmos to accelerate.

More recently, based on massive datasets gleaned from the Hubble Space Telescope, researchers are now wrestling with a new cosmic anomaly. It appears like something's causing the universe to fly apart even more quickly than previously calculated, faster than current dark energy calculations can explain away. The ever-creative astronomers are considering calling this new interstellar head-scratcher *early dark energy*. Related findings may require altering the estimated age of the universe from

13.8 billion years to a more youthful thirteen billion.

Johns Hopkins University astronomer Adam Riess led the research on our latest galactic conundrum. He reported, "The universe seems to throw a lot of surprises at us, and that's a good thing, because it helps us learn."

And that seems like a healthy mindset for life in general: sometimes you win; sometimes you learn.

Unfortunately, though, our species appears to be riddled with slow learners.

The entire planet was pummeled for well over two years by the COVID-19 pandemic. Some of its lessons seem so clear yet remain unlearned by so many.

- **Lesson 1:** *Everything is connected.* Somebody coughs in South Africa, and Broadway shows close in New York City.
- **Lesson 2:** *Security is a fiction.* You can lose

your health, wealth, loved ones, and daily routine at the drop of a hat.

- **Lesson 3:** *Humankind isn't as dominant and powerful as some might like to think.* Our entire race has been chastened by a submicroscopic collection of genetic code encased in a small coat of protein.

From this perspective, the pandemic sometimes seemed like a worldwide remedial school delivering a mandatory crash-course curriculum in interconnection, impermanence, and humility.

So what to do?

Some look to science. Science helps us acquire the knowledge necessary to address many complex problems. We've come a long way since first adopting the scientific method. That practice started sometime around the seventeenth century grounded by the precepts of studious observation, empirical analysis, objective interpretation, and heavy doses of skepticism.

Skepticism rocks. I'll take doubt over dogma any day of the week.

But science doesn't have the answers to everything. Maybe it never will. Uncertainty persists in so many aspects of life.

Still, there are those who believe that science will figure *everything* out someday in the future. Is this belief a kind of faith? Maybe that might explain why some refer to science as our modern-day religion. Although that seems somewhat like a false equivalency.

Others look to religion for answers to life's big questions. In return, those folks may get more than a smattering of bullshittery wrapped up in easy-to-digest answers.

Whatever works. If religiousness helps some people grow in wisdom and learn to love better, then that may be a prudent path for them — if only for a while.

In a poem titled "Go to the Limits of Your Longing," Rainer Maria Rilke wrote the following lines:

Let everything happen to you: beauty and terror.
Just keep going.
No feeling is final.

Life is full of beauty and terror—and everything else in between. Precious and precarious. Transience may be the only thing that never changes.

OK, maybe that and the speed of light.

EPILOGUE

Like life, this book must end.

If you've made it this far, you'll recognize my favorite and most repeated phrase:

I don't know.

But looking back, maybe those words aren't entirely true.

I know this:

**I'm fortunate and grateful to be
living the mystery.**

Made in the USA
Monee, IL
06 August 2022

11060687R00083